'If there is one person who is eminently qualified to write about luxury, it is Mahul.'

– Bibek Debroy, Chairman, PM Economic Advisory Council

Luxe Inferno

Dr. Mahul Brahma

Book Three of The Luxe Trilogy

ASIN: B084FB7R9R

ISBN: 9798608035708

Cover Design and author photograph:

Ms Sabiya Sinha Roy

Cover Painting: Mr Pranab Roy

All illustrations by the author

About the author

Dr Mahul Brahma is a luxury commentator, columnist and author of 'The Luxe Trilogy', which comprises three books – *Decoding Luxe*, *Dark Luxe* and *Luxe Inferno*.

Dr Brahma is a columnist on luxury with leading national newspaper *DNA,* and has earlier been writing for *The Economic Times*. He has worked as Senior Editor and in several other capacities with leading media houses such as *The Economic Times, DNA*, India partner of *New York Times*, CNBC TV 18 group and Reuters.

He is an award-winning leader in communications, CSR, digital marketing, branding. He heads CSR, Corporate Communications and Branding in a Tata group company, mjunction.

Dr Brahma has won several national-level awards in communication and CSR, including Best Communication Strategist of the Year Award in 2019, CSR Leader of the Year Award in 2019, Brand Leadership Award in 2017, Ecommerce Communication Leader of the Year

Award in 2017, and Young Achiever Award in National Awards for Excellence in Corporate Communications in 2016.

His short films were selected and screened at prestigious film festivals like Cannes Film Festival, Berlin Short Film Festival and Dada Saheb Phalke Film Festival.

He is an alumnus of St Xavier's College (Calcutta), SSSUTMS, MICA (Ahmedabad), IIM Calcutta, and University of Cambridge - Judge Business School.

Dr Brahma is an artist and loves to play golf.

Wikipedia: https://en.wikipedia.org/wiki/Mahul _Brahma

Website: www.mahulbrahma.com

Facebook: @AuthorMahul

Twitter: @mahulbrahma

Instagram: @mahulbrahma

Praise for the author and 'The Luxe Trilogy':

"Wishing Mahul all the success in all that he endeavours."

– Amitabh Bachchan

"I wish Mahul's book all the success."

– Ratan N. Tata

"Let more writings come through the pen of Mahul."

– Keshari Nath Tripathi, Hon. Governor of West Bengal (Former)

"You and your writings always have all my blessings Mahul."

– Mamata Banerjee, Hon Chief Minister of West Bengal

"Congratulations and best wishes for your new book, Mahul!"

– Harish Bhat, Author, Brand Custodian of Tata Sons

"The romance of luxury has waited long for such a deft rendition of insight and eloquence."

– Kunal Basu, Author

"A quiet voice that will have a thundering impact. An essential read."

> — *Sarnath Banerjee, Graphic Novelist,*
> *Author*

"I love the way Mahul deconstructs the mystical world of luxury with his simple, direct, matter-of-fact lucid style of narration.

> – *Arnab Chakraborty, National Director, UN-*
> *Empretec Programme for India*

This book is dedicated to immortal creations --

'Divina Commedia' by Dante Alighieri and 'Mappa dell'Inferno' by Sandro Botticelli.

Acknowledgement

Dear Reader, I thank you for your trust in this humble story-teller.

A sincere thanks to Dante Alighieri and his immortal creation *The Divine Comedy* and to Sandro Botticelli for his rendition of the Inferno.

Thanks to Mr Amitabh Bachchan and Mr Ratan Tata for your kind words and support.

A big thanks to Bibek da (Debroy) for the brilliant foreword.

Thanks to Pranab sir for the beautiful rendition of Botticelli's Map of Hell.

Thanks to my family and better half Sabiya for your love and encouragement. It would not have been possible without you.

God has been very kind.

Dr. Mahul Brahma

Contents

Foreword

The word "deluxe" means we are talking about luxury. The average person loves luxury, even if the pleasure is vicarious. I remember watching a behavioral experiment in a museum. The museum had a chair and you could pay $10 for the privilege of sitting on it. There weren't too many takers willing to pay $10 for the privilege of sitting on a perfectly ordinary-looking chair. The museum then cordoned off the chair behind some ropes and put up a sign saying, "So and so (a celebrity) sat on this chair." Immediately, there was a queue of people willing to pay the price. The chair had acquired a value that surpassed the price. It had become a luxury item. Thorstein Veblen and John Kenneth Galbraith would have scoffed at such instances of conspicuous consumption. However, "deluxe" is a fact of life. The dingiest of barbers will have a sign that proclaims, "Deluxe hair-cutting saloon".

Not all deluxe is dingy. The use of the word does connote branding and quality. Who better than Dr. Mahul Brahma to educate us about deluxe? He has been writing on the subject for decades, and he has now given us *Luxe Inferno*, the third installment of 'The Luxe Trilogy'. The first book *Decoding Luxe* is about the dazzle. It explains to the reader what deluxe means, with plenty of examples and anecdotes from the early 1900s. In case it hasn't registered, there is fake or counterfeit deluxe too.

The second book of the trilogy *Dark Luxe* is rather unusual, since it is about the dark. Deluxe is inexorably intertwined with crime. While the first book was about fact, the second book is fiction. The third sub-group, which is used in this book, is a medley of this and that. Perhaps one can call it *faction*.

If you like luxury and deluxe, you will like this book. If not, you are a cynic. I am alluding to the famous Oscar Wilde quote from *Lady Windermere's Fan*: A cynic is "A man who knows the price of everything, and the value of nothing."

We forget what Cecil Graham said in response to Lord Darlington. "And a sentimentalist, my dear Darlington, is a man who sees an absurd value in everything and doesn't know the market price of any single thing." You need to be a sentimentalist to appreciate deluxe and this book.

Dr. Bibek Debroy

Chairman, Prime Minister's Economic Advisory Council

Author's note on 'The Luxe Trilogy'

Dear Reader,

Luxe Inferno is a philosophical quest for the true meaning of luxury. It has two parts which captures a mix of Yin and Yang of luxury. The first part is fiction and narrates a philosophical story of a luxe-o-holic through the nine circles of inferno of luxe, taking him to the Purgatory or may be the Paradiso. But whether he will be successful in his pursuit, I leave it to you, my discerning reader, to infer. The second part comprises commentary based on my research that spans over a decade. It explores the various facets of this dynamic subject of luxury classified into three segments – strategy, brands and perception. This is a very unique mix of fiction and non-fiction, or 'faction', exploring the depths of the inferno as well as the heights of dazzle.

In The Luxe Trilogy, all the books are separate reads and have their independent identities. The Trilogy comprises *Decoding Luxe, Dark Luxe* and *Luxe Inferno. Decoding Luxe* traces the history of evolution of luxury from the time of the Maharajas, giving a strategic perspective to the subject and a deeper understanding beyond the myopic concept of price tag-luxury. *Dark Luxe*, on the other hand, is an anthology of 13 short stories on luxury and crime, dealing with the darkness that hides behind the veil of luxury. It gives you a peek into the depths to which human minds can reach, luxury being a silent witness and sometimes accessory. The first book is a work of non-fiction and the second fiction. The third book, *Luxe Inferno* has a more philosophical approach towards this subject. It is a journey deep into the human mind and its labyrinths.

While each of these books hold their own and are independent reads, together they carve out a holistic story of luxe – stories, written as fiction, non-fiction and 'faction'.

This story takes readers on a voyage to the heights of opulence as well as the depths of inferno. The idea also is to make luxury an academic discourse, therefore making it inclusive, instead of the exclusivity and myopia it has shrouded itself with.

Books on luxury have never moved beyond 'price tags' and thus have never done justice to the subject.

The Luxe Trilogy, thus in its own unique way, narrates a complete story of luxe.

Dr. Mahul Brahma

Prologue

Luxe is all about perceptions

The fun fact about luxe is that if it looks expensive, it surely is.

The luxury industry runs on creating perceptions, one after the other, where each one tries to topple another. Brand custodians all over the world have sleepless nights in creating these perceptions and then creating some more. It is the primary preoccupation of the dream merchants in the luxury industry. It is the perception that justifies the steep premium paid by price-sensitive Indian customers.

Branding luxe is all about conjuring beautiful and fanciful images in the minds of the customers. And so every luxury brand prefers to conjure some magic – a perception. "Most expensive" as a tag that customers drool over, is certainly not easy to get. The natural corollary to this tag is - why is it so expensive? So it won't matter if you just keep hiking your price; there has to be a demand created for it. Perception is the key element is creating this demand. So let me take you through three key strategic perception-enablers that luxury brands have been exploiting since the beginning of time and will surely keep exploiting till the end of time.

Razzle Dazzle: Remember that news of Azzam, the largest yacht in the world, or the diamond and ruby-studded 24-carat gold bodied Rolls Royce Phantom, or the most expensive wine Domaine de la Romanée-Conti or DRC ($551,314), or the most expensive bottled water Beverly Hills 90H20 Luxy Collection Diamond Edition ($100,000 per bottle), or Saluki, the most expensive dog ($5,000). These are the stuff that dreams are made of, and they create the "world's most expensive" perceptions. This razzle-dazzle is the quickest and easiest means of creating a perception to conjure dreams that make spending millions and billions sound so justified.

Rarity: This is a very potent key to creating perception that can make people loosen their purse strings. The perception of rarity can be classified into two categories:

i) Ancient artefacts made by artisans who are no longer alive, paintings or sculptures by greats like Leonardo Da Vinci or Michelangelo, or an object, say a writing instrument or a watch used by a famous personality who is no longer alive (like Napolean Bonaparte or Mahatma Gandhi). Take for instance the priceless death mask of King Tut. These artefacts, paintings or writing instruments or watches were not rare when these well-known figures were alive; they never fetched billions at Sotheby's. Most of the great artists such as Vincent van Gogh died penniless while now their art is fetching billions of dollars. Blame it on the perception of rarity!

ii) When a watchman tries to create a complicated mechanism like a tourbillon that will give precision to a mechanical watch, this is rarity. Every such rare watch, such rare mechanical movement is painstakingly crafted by masters over months and may be years. Such pieces are rare. This is same for any artefact or a piece of art. The man hours put into its creation give the perception of rarity to these objects.

Exclusivity: Every individual longs to be special and not ordinary. They want to receive special treatment, they want to be looked up to and envied. They desire to be emulated, they desire to belong to a certain club of exclusivity where entry in by invitation only. Luxury brands like Rolex and Louis Vuitton rely heavily on this enabler. If you own a Rolex, you will "live for greatness" and be an integral of an exclusive notional club of all owners of Rolex, such as President John F Kennedy or Martin Luther King Junior, or even tennis star Roger Federer. Or Louis Vuitton telling you if you own their trunks or duffle bags, then you will know that "there are journeys that turn into legends", which a famous ad campaign featuring "Core values" of the LV brand with Sir Sean Connery, Bono, Francis Ford Coppola and Angelina Jolie. This is selling the perception of rising beyond the ordinary, becoming exclusive.

Part A

LUXE INFERNO

'All hope abandon, ye who enter here'

'The more a thing is perfect, the more it feels pleasure and pain.'

Chapter 1

Love at first sight

If you are a business journalist, very soon in the profession, you develop an immunity towards large financial numbers. So much so that you develop an apathy towards figures which are less than nine or ten zeroes. The rationale being that, these figures, do not make headlines. This attitude gives clarity in terms of how not to be awed by multiple zeroes. When you report or edit, you do that without any awe or disdain.

It was after a few years of hard core business journalism that our protagonist, D, or let's say, 'Dante', got an opportunity to explore the feature side of business. A newspaper was launched which decided to bring out a magazine on luxury brands. The Editor-in-Chief, V, or, let's say 'Virgil', told Dante it will be a great opportunity for him to explore this wonderful world of luxury.

Virgil had been a feature writer all his life and thus had limited understanding of hard core news. Dante, on the other hand, was a hard-core news person and was not convinced that he would enjoy the so-called 'lighter side of business journalism'. But Virgil was determined and started narrating stories of his adventures in covering features and how it was a great learning experience. What Dante thought he would miss the most was the adrenaline rush that came with hard news. Dante liked Virgil's style, his love for finer things of life and his love for branded luxury. From his training as a hard-core journalist, he thought Virgil's flaunting of luxury brands was quite shallow. However, at some level, Dante too, felt good about the finer things of life.

Dante agreed to take on the job, but couldn't help but ask Virgil, "Why me? I am a very blunt instrument. Getting news from tough cookies comes more easily to me than appreciating fine craftsmanship."

Virgil smiled and said, "Welcome to the world of luxury."

Dante quickly retorted, "The world of luxe."

Virgil said, "Lux? The soap?"

Dante replied, "Luxe with an 'e'. This means 'dazzle' and is the origin of the word 'luxury'.

You see, there are a few advantages of being a good quizzer."

The days ahead of a newspaper launch are like a roller coaster ride, high on adrenaline. No fixed timings, no office norms, no punching in or out. You come in at your own time and leave whenever you feel like. Or stay back. It is a cycle of intense planning and then execution, only to be dismantled the next moment. Just like a Jacques Derrida's 'Theory of Deconstruction', life goes on destroying and creating, in a rhythm. Dante's challenge was to understand luxury in the midst of this chaos. He started researching on the subject and very soon realized that there was no literature on luxe or luxury. All the writings had been mere product reviews with "price of request" tags and high resolution pictures. That is all. Dante was in a spot. He was too proud to ask Virgil for a way out as he had taken it up as a personal challenge.

It was his day off and Dante decided to pay a visit to the newly-opened luxury mall in town. He was not one to give in to shopping, so mall visits were rare. Not a fan. Days off were few and far between, with the deadline pressure of the launch, but even the rare ones were spent mostly reading.

This trip was purely for academic purpose. To get a feel of luxe. The mall was a little different from the usual ones. Quite decently designed, and the best thing was, quite dignified and not in your face, like the others in the city.

Dante had decided that the first day will be for observation; some window shopping to get a feel of the luxury brands, the visual merchandise, but most importantly, to watch the buyers – and their reaction to luxe!

The first was a Louis Vuitton boutique. He first spotted a beautiful trunk which was on display. The design of the truck was beautiful, the stitches were exquisite and the vintage touch had a very alluring feel. He could not stop himself, and went near it. He started to closely observe the trunk, which was genuinely old and was like a fine piece of art. He thought he was in a gallery, appreciating a classic. As an artist, how could he not appreciate art? And what was in front of him was pure art! The boutique manager walked up to him, smiled and said, "In 1928, the Maharaja of Jammu & Kashmir placed orders for custom-made thirty trunks with us. This one was recently donated to us by the family. LV had customized it for the Maharaja. Talking of LV trunks, let me share some more interesting facets of this long and loving courtship of LV with Indian Royalty. Sir, Louis Vuitton was unique in use of valuable materials and precious leathers. The luxury house was always able to serve special requests from the Indian Maharajas, no matter how extraordinary, elaborate or detailed the demands were. A certain Maharaja had ordered all the trunks imaginable for the most diverse of items – golf clubs, turbans, decorations, polo sticks, horseshoes, colonial helmets, among others."

Dante didn't realize how time went by; he was completely engrossed by Karthik's story. Dante smiled and introduced himself as a journalist who wrote on luxury. Karthik seemed happy with the introduction and offered him tea and continued with his story. Dante spent the next forty-five minutes in the boutique.

It was love at first sight.

Karthik ushered him to the door and asked him to visit again. In this whole story telling session, things happened like magic. Dante just fell in love with the brand, the story, the legacy and desperately wanted to be a part of it. Small wonder, he swiped his card and left the store with an LV monogrammed, hand-stitched sling. Stories can be addictive.

It was Dante's first luxury purchase. He was elated. He now owned a bit of luxe. He visited the Cartier boutique next, while observing the old photographs adorning the Trinity necklaces, the manager Azam walked up to him and noticing the keen interest, decided to share a story. Sir, in 1926, the Maharaja of Patiala commissioned us, Cartier, our largest till date, to remodel his crown jewels, which included the 234.69 carat De Beers diamond. The result was a breath-taking Patiala necklace weighing 962.25 carats with 2,930 diamonds. He pointed towards the picture of the Maharaja adorning the crown necklace. Dante introduced himself. Azam was happy to share more interesting stories over a cup of tea. He took Dante though the collection, explaining the exquisite craftsmanship and the rarity of the products. One discussion led to another and Dante made his second luxe purchase of the day. A golden lighter, Cartier's special edition.

Much later, he realized that he did not smoke.
But no worries, it was a day that was
special…and unique.

Dante was in love with luxe.

'To rear me was the task of power divine,
Supremest wisdom, and primeval love.'

Chapter 2

The Power

It was baptism by fire for Dante. His two purchases – which would wipe out a major part of his salary when the credit card bill would be due – had now made him a part of the elite and exclusive clubs of two iconic luxury brands. He was so happy, so engrossed into the two items. He was very eager to show them to Virgil. Moreover, he had two very interesting stories which had given him much food for thought. These stories had opened up a new channel to approach luxury…stories. These stories, in most of the cases, were factual, with a dash of fiction and folklore. That's how his quest began in search of stories behind luxe.

Intense research followed and the one that topped his list was of a remarkable and marquee brand – Rolls Royce. He planned to share this story with Virgil over their smoking sessions. Dante was a passive smoker earlier, but the Cartier gold limited edition lighter, he thought, demanded that he started smoking, and an expensive brand at that! Virgil took out his

Charminar and before he could take out his
match box, Dante quickly lighted it up with his
new acquisition. Virgil was taken aback. To his
surprise, Dante took out a Marlboro and lighted
it up, taking a long and delayed puff. Virgil took
the lighter from him and examined it with keen
eyes. He was very surprised as the lighter was
pretty expensive and he never thought Dante
would actually end up buying such an expensive
lighter. The game had begun!

Dante smiled and said, "Isn't she a beauty?
This was the last piece, made in France."
Without further ado, Dante started sharing
his story of the Rolls Royce. "You know Virgil,
in 1920s, 25% of Rolls Royce sales used to
come from India alone. Luxury has a long lost
history with our Royalty. Let me share a story
with you about Maharaja Jai Singh of Alwar,
who brought this iconic company to its knees.

"He was visiting London. On one of his evening
walks in plain English clothes, while passing a
Rolls Royce showroom, he decided to go inside
and asked the manager about the specifications
of the cars, their prices and requested a test
drive. The manager just saw an Indian and

ignored his request, and went so far as to rudely show the Maharaja the door.

"This treatment naturally made him furious. Jai Singh got back to his hotel and asked for an official visit of the Indian king to the Rolls Royce showroom to be arranged. When he appeared in his formal outfit, dressed in sparkling clothes and jewellery, the Maharaja was welcomed with a red carpet and employees standing on both sides of it paying their respects to the king."

"Jai Singh spent more than two hours in the showroom, trying all the six latest models exhibited. In the end, he purchased all of the cars in the showroom. He paid for them all right away, including the costs of delivery.

"When the cars reached India, he converted them into garbage collectors. This was his revenge. When the word got out, Rolls Royce sent numerous apologies to the Maharaja, but this blemish will stay with Rolls till the brand exists."

Dante took a pause and put out his Marlboro.

While Virgil was listening to this interesting story, his mind and attention was somewhat stuck at the Cartier lighter. He, as editor, had been the sole 'connoisseur' of luxury till now. And while he was using a match, Dante was flaunting a Cartier! "Am I paying him too much?" he wondered to himself.

He did not let it show, but somewhere deep down, he started regretting giving Dante the responsibility of the luxury magazine. He, at some level, did want to expose Dante to luxury and was confident that he would appreciate the world of luxury. But in all this he thought, he being the one to introduce him to this new world, would always remain the last word. He had forgotten that the things he loved about Dante, for which he had trusted him with a new subject and hired him, was his dedication and passion. He consoled himself and thought it might just have been the initial excitement that he took a step forward and actually bought these luxury goods (he had also noticed the LV monogrammed bag by then).

Dante was a keen observer. He did notice a slight change in Virgil's look. He enjoyed the game. These brands made him feel a power that he had never felt before. It was alluring.

'The mind which is created quick to love,

Is responsive to everything that is pleasing,

Soon as by pleasure it is awakened into activity.'

Chapter 3

The New Identity

Branded luxury gave Dante a new high. So with the new-found power, he set sail on a new adventure. Little did he know that his encounter with Virgil was the first step towards 'Limbo', or the first circle of Luxe Inferno. Eight more circles to go till he reaches the centre of the inferno.

The problem with high is that it is addictive. And ironically, plastic money, rather credit card, plays a very significant role.

The trips to the luxury mall became more frequent. In most cases, it was just in search of more stories. And his new friends, the boutique managers, were very happy to see him and chat with him. For them, there were hardly any customers who took interest in the history of these luxury brands. So it was always either a hard sale, trying to establish the value for money, or a quick one, wherein the customer exactly knew what he or she wanted and thus made a quick purchase without even exchanging pleasantries. With his exploring new brands, his friend circle also started expanding.

Soon, Dante realized that luxury, especially branded luxury, was an integral part of one's identity. He started noticing brands people around him wore. The watch, the shoes, the jacket, the glasses, the writing instruments, the car... he started closely watching every element of brand presence in an individual. This was a new facet that he had hitherto ignored completely. For Dante, all the other facets still remained important, but somehow, this one started rising the ranks. He soon realized that there are four types of luxury consumers – ranging from a category that shamelessly flaunt the brands to the ones who are very private with their collection. So he decided to write an analysis classifying the consumers in the debut edition of the luxury magazine. Little did he realize how his own identity has transformed and reduced to the brands he used – Cartier lighter, Montblanc pens, Louis Vuitton bags, Gucci glasses, Salvatore Ferragamo shoes, and Armani shirts. Here are some edited excerpts of the debut article:

First, the Experientialists

This genre typically values new and exciting experiences, more than buying products or brands. They lavishly spend on experiences. In their structured lives, they seek a getaway, hence five star hotel stays, fine dining or adventurous/thrilling experiences are their poison. Luxury to them brings up images of being suspended in time and space, not having the pressures of daily life and work responsibilities as they enjoy the time away.

An exquisite piece of art or a handcrafted timepiece may also give a similar experience when you are just in a space where you are appreciating the beauty of it. It is a time warp; every time you look at it, you become so mesmerised by the beauty that you forget your meetings and deadlines. The experience is the luxury, the experience is the dazzle or luxe.

Personalisation of experiences takes luxury to a new level. It's no longer personalisation of menus at fine diners for the elite; it could even include the name of the customer being printed on the menu. So for an experientialist, this is value for money. Going forward, these discerning consumers would like to stay in specialty boutique hotels or resorts, luxury spas or private apartments and villas, when on a holiday.

Now let's meet the Connoisseurs

This genre is passionate in certain areas of interest and is mostly well-informed and knowledgeable about it. These could be art, scotch, wine, watches, writing instruments, cigars, horses, not particularly in that order. These connoisseurs get together and appreciate the finer aspects of their passion. They form clubs and meet for a quiet appreciation of the finer things in life. It may be a Horology Society of time-keepers or a Wine Club or a Cuban Cigar Club or a Super Car Club.

This segment just revels in enjoying what they appreciate the most. For instance, the Single Malt Club members come together, discuss, study, debate and share their appreciation and experience in high spirits (pun intended).

They will spend their time and money in pursuit of the collection of personal passion points. They make the pursuit of their area of passion a mission and pursue it with zest and will not bat an eyelid before spending a fortune on limited editions, or handcrafted editions, or the spirit of the bygone era.

They are reluctant to place value on brands unless it stands for exquisite exclusivity. They take pride in their knowledge of esoteric brands that are not widely known. Luxury to them is purely a matter of the level of craftsmanship, the number of man hours spent, which will determine the quality of the products or services that they buy. Niche, but specialised brands across categories will make their mark with these consumers. They are willing to pay a higher premium, so curated services that bring such products to them will be a great getaway to tap into their need for excellence.

The next segment is the life force that drives luxury in India.

Meet the Flaunters

A socialite friend who used to swear by a clutch that she used to take to every party had secretly confessed that she isn't that fond of it but only carries it for the monogram tag. That's the power of a brand for this category.

Welcome to the world of flaunters, who tend to value brand name over all other factors. The visibility of the brand name at strategic positions across the product is a big deal for them, as such purchases denote their status in their society. So the brand needs to be aspirational, else, what's the big deal? The newly-rich or new money classes, especially their younger counterparts, are mostly badge-seekers at the stage where the brand name is supposedly the biggest status indicator. There is a strong urge to prove to the society that they are also a part of the elitist luxury brand-wagon.

According to a survey, more such consumers were seen in cities like Ludhiana, where they justify the ownership of brands by stating that they are now in a status or position which makes it de rigueur. Interestingly, for this category of consumers, the brands are on a continuum. They can show off Zara as a daily wear to Prada on special occasions with élan.

As flaunters move up the societal ladder, the badge value is conferred not only by the brand, but also by the level of difficulty in obtaining the product or service. Dinner reservation at hard-to-get restaurants, Birkin or Kelly bags for which the wait list is over four years, monogrammed and hot stamped Louis Vuitton bags with their initials, accessories made from exotic leather like of crocodile or snake – the ability to acquire these with relative ease is a reflection of their status.

To tap this segment of consumers, well known but exclusive services and products are the way forward.

And last but not the least, I present to you the Aesthetes
To this category of people, the brand is much less important than the design. Aesthetes are luxury consumers purely because they have arrived at a stage of income due to which they can indulge in their love for design among luxury brands or products.
They will shell out a bomb because the object of desire is hand-stitched and not because of the label. They pride themselves for having an eye that picks up the unique and bold in design.

The difference between them and the connoisseur is that the latter has certain passions which they follow with zeal. Quality and craftsmanship are very important for the connoisseurs, however, for the former category, it is the aesthetic appeal, the look, the intricacies of the design that appeal to their senses. They are also likely to pursue this aesthetic across categories, unlike a connoisseur.

Aesthetes and Flaunters are on the opposite ends of the spectrum. While Aesthetes are obsessed with design, and label or logo comes quite low on the priority list, for Flaunters, label or logo comes right on top and design takes a backseat. However, even Aesthetes are Flaunters in a way; they also flaunt their exquisite designs and feel pride at the snob quotient that most people are not even able to understand or appreciate the elegance. They feel exclusive.

'If the present world goes astray,
the cause is in you,

In you it is to be sought.'

Chapter 4

The Clash

So, which category was Dante? Was he a flaunter at heart thinking he was a connoisseur? Or the other way round. There were clearly two levels of his consumption – one was the increasing need for establishing an identity based on branded luxury and the other was purely academic, for the magazine.

While his consumption classification was still a matter of debate, there was one development that he couldn't help but notice – Virgil was slowly but steadily transforming into a 'flaunter' from a 'connoisseur'. Also, every other day, he was busy showing off his 'acquisition' of the latest collection of a luxury brand. A more interesting news came in when one of his friends at the mall told him that Virgil has also enquired about Dante and what he had recently bought.

Dante did not take it well. There was a very wide gap between his and Virgil's salaries. He was in his fifties and Dante was just 27. But

Dante was no quitter. He realized it was time to up his game. He needed a new high, beating Virgil in brand one-upmanship. His credit card bills were pinching quite hard, but it was a matter of the three-lettered word that drives luxury – EGO.

So, as per the advice of his relationship manager, he converted the credit card bill into EMIs against a steep monthly interest. And predictably, slowly, the flaunting game turned into a battle. From a buyer of stories, Dante became a "prized patron" of a few luxury brands, so much so, he was offered steady discounts and sneak peeks into private collections of these luxury brands.

His collection swelled and so did his EMIs. Virgil failed to contain his displeasure at being challenged in this luxury flaunting game. No one could remove him from his luxury connoisseur throne, certainly not a 20-something. His anger slipped into the professional arena and he started venting out his anger on Dante at work, picking on issues just to put him down, show him who was the boss. Virgil had anger management issues and was quite known for his shouting sprees. But Dante, with his newfound power and identity and fully aware of the actual reason behind change in Virgil's behaviour, decided not to back down.

The newsroom witnessed their clashes very frequently. Eventually, every clash boiled down to one question – who was the bigger authority or connoisseur on luxury.

He realized that his salary was not enough as Virgil's war chest was pretty huge. He felt so compelled that even against his wish, just in order to garner borrowed funds from his friends and colleagues, he started lying about his father's health. He hated himself for doing it. He loved his father very much. But this was his last resort. He could not quit the game.

Little did he realize that over the next few months, he would be consumed by his deadly sins and would slowly move deeper from Upper Hell to Lower Hell, steadily running towards the 9th or innermost circle.

'O human race, born to fly upward,

wherefore at a little wind dost thou
so fall?'

Chapter 5

To Hell and Back

One year passed by; Dante and Virgil's one-upmanship game only increased its intensity. It had grown from brands, to the latest collections of the same brands. Dante was completely hooked on to the game, its addiction, and was enjoying it thoroughly. His status in the organization had also elevated as he was directly pitted against the Editor-in-Chief. Another bone of contention was the fact that in lieu of his day-to-day writings on luxury brands, he had to meet many CXOs of these luxury brands, which increased his network as well as knowledge of these brands and also resulted in invitations to visit their headquarters in Switzerland or Dubai. These interactions helped him get a deeper insight into the brand story, which he later penned down in his book. So, to these luxury brand CXOs, Dante became the face of the paper, and not Virgil.

Even with the rising clashes and credit card dues as well as borrowings, life was good. Dante was moving from one high to another. He was totally consumed by the addiction.

But one phone call changed everything. His father was diagnosed with cancer at an Advanced stage.

There was a sudden need for cash, as then cancer was not covered under the company's insurance policy. He was earning very decently and could have saved enough for an emergency even after continuing his existing standard of living. The keyword is "could have" because he "could not". His savings were zilch, rather negative. All he had were 10 wallets, 12 slings, 8 watches, 15 writing instruments and the list went on. If you calculate the total money spent on these labels, it could jolly well take care of the medical expense. But these were of no use now. Just no use at all. The worst hit was when he realized that his EMI was consuming more than half his salary. And there was no asset against it, neither a house nor a car, which he could sell off.

He was completely helpless with the credit card EMIs and the money borrowed. He had no idea from where he would get the money to treat his ailing father.

A sudden realization dawned on him. What was the point of all this? It was just a game of one-upmanship that led to this disaster. From an upstart journalist, today he stood almost a pauper where his greed had made him incapable of supporting his father during this time of need.

He cursed the day he had first borrowed money from his close friend Suresh, citing his father's ill-health as an excuse. He could not forgive himself for that. Was it bad karma and was his father was paying the price?

He realized he was in the centre of Luxe Inferno where the Devil himself resides.

He had committed treason against his father with the lie.

He needed to come back from this hell and help his dying father or kill himself in this inferno.

All this while, he was justifying his addiction with academic interest. He loved the subject, but the seven sins took him to the dark side of luxe, inside this rabbit hole. Now, he regretted his addiction, he regretted his entire journey through the nine circles of the inferno.

But he had to come back; he had to come back for his father.

'Consider your origin.

You were not formed to live like brutes

but to follow virtue and knowledge.'

Chapter 6

The Paradiso

Luxury is just like science or technology; it is as good and as bad as the user makes of it. If the sins of humans decide to take luxury to the bottomless pit of hell, it is very easy. It is also easy to enjoy the subject and the learnings and not be addicted to it, not to identify with it. Once the latter approach is taken, we realize that luxury – or rather branded luxury – is not who we are; it is not our identity, it is what dream merchants want us to believe. The essence of luxury needs to be savoured slowly, enjoyed like a good book or like a memorable journey, and all the while keeping your identity intact.

Dante knew that his addiction was supported by two things which needed to be severed immediately – Virgil and his one-upmanship with him, as well as the city that hailed this blatant showcasing and flaunting of luxury brands.

The next morning, he bid Virgil goodbye, quit the job and the city for good, to be with his father. He quit the game. In the next few weeks, he managed to sell most of his prized possessions and pay his debt. It was his moment of clarity, his nirvana.

On the other hand, Virgil was relieved that he would again reclaim his title as the luxury connoisseur. A part of him, however, missed Dante and the game, especially the adrenaline rush. But very soon he found a new Dante and continued a new game with her. To Virgil, the inferno was an infinite loop from which he could never transcend.

The journey to hell and back had given Dante a perspective of luxe and luxury that was rare and had put him in a very advantageous position as a writer. He decided to pen his thoughts and perspectives and take it to a wider audience so that people could understand luxury beyond the "price tag". He started writing columns on luxury for a few foreign publications and sharing his ideas in various forums, which helped him take care of the expenses of his father's cancer treatment. Dante realized luxury was a much wider subject and to understand it one needed to understand both the dazzle and the darkness that hides behind it.

One day, when he was telling his father how this one-upmanship has dearly cost him as well as Virgil, Dante's father laughed and narrated a story. He said, during the time of Zamindars in Bengal, one-upmanship was very common. There were two neighbouring Zamindars who were almost at war with each other over this never-ending competition – who is superior. So when one day Zamindar A purchased and showcased his new imported two-horse driven Phaeton, Zamindar B got jealous. Within a week, he bought and showcased a four-horse driven imported Phaeton. A got very jealous and increased the number of horses by two, B retaliated by increasing it further. A took a step forward and replaced the horses by two zebras. This was the first zebra-driven Phaeton in Calcutta. They both laughed and the story helped Dante unburden his guilt a bit.

A year had passed, but his father's condition had still not improved. For over a year, he had not made any luxury purchase. He had sold most of his luxury belongings and even gave away a few to his friends.

His writings were well accepted by audience and looked beyond any myopic view of luxury, tracing its evolution and how it has manifested itself in today's world.

The moment he ceased being a luxe-o-holic, freeing himself from the addiction, he fell in love with luxe.

The purgatory of life had made him live with death and a fear of losing his father to a deadly disease every moment, regretting his journey to Luxe Inferno.

One day when the doctor told him that the final days of his father were nearing, Dante broke into tears. His father was a strong man. He told him, "Son, life is short and I have lived a full life. I have no regrets as I have you by my side. I want you to understand that every experience – good or bad – was God's way of teaching you to pass in this exam called life. His objective is not to kill you, but to make you stronger. So your experience with luxury and the sins which took you to hell and back was necessary. Life has been your purgatory and you are now wiser and stronger. It has given you a purpose. So always know that god has been very kind and thank him."

After a few days, his father passed away. He tried to remain strong, but broke down into tears intermittently. He was not able to contain his emotions. The loss was unbearable. It was a very deep wound, a gift from his inferno, which changed something deep within him. It was a throbbing pain. Unbearable. Intermittently, he felt the urge to relieve himself of this pain, to liberate the wound. To accept that change and liberate himself. He had picked up the razor a few times, taken it close to his wrist, made the cold steel touch the vein and feel the throbbing pulse. More than once, he had been convinced this was the only way to relieve himself of the pain, to escape this hell, to purgate himself. His sins took away his father. He could never forgive himself.

But then, he could hear his father's last words, "…life has been your purgatory and you are now wiser and stronger."

Dante has to rise from his ashes like a phoenix, for his father's sake.

Would the Luxe Inferno ever set him free?

Would he ever see the Paradiso?

"We're all in the same game; just different levels.

Dealing with the same hell, just different devils." – Anonymous

Lucifer

*'Into the eternal darkness, into fire
and into ice.'*

Part B

I: Strategy

Chapter 1

Golden rules for creating luxe aura

The multi-billion-dollar question that worries every brand custodians is – what is the right strategy to brand a luxury product or service? Let us see how luxury branding is different, and take you through the golden rules that need to be followed to make a luxury product or service withstand the test of time.

These tenets are:

1. Selling legacy;

2. Creating aspiration;

3. Creating exclusivity;

4. Customisation;

5. Understanding the history and culture of target geography;

6. EMOD - Every point of contact needs to be trained well to handle customers;

7. Keeping brand promise;

8. Making the 'haves' feel special;

9. Never forgetting the have-nots;

10. Targeted marketing and communicating of luxe stories.

When a Rolex advertisement showcases that the legendary US President JFK used to sport the watch, it sends a message to the target customers – you are a part of legacy. Brands like Louis Vuitton, Rolex, IWC and Montblanc have been successfully harnessing this "legacy quotient" to get more and more customers. These watches or writing instruments or luggage crafters charge a hefty premium because of the legacy quotient, which just money can't buy. You have to be worth it. It is a very smart strategy to establish aspiration, which creates a pull towards a product or service – something that's beyond the price tag and dazzles you. It is critical for a brand to evoke aspiration, which, like legacy, gives a sense of exclusivity. A brand custodian needs to keep this key element in mind while crafting the brand story. It is this sense of being a part of an elite group that lures buyers and makes them loosen their purse strings. If by buying a luxury product or service a customer gets a feeling that only money is the differential factor, then he or she will feel insecure that anyone will be allowed in this so-called 'exclusive club' if they have the moolah. This feeling of exclusivity creates loyalty.

In today's global village, every brand is looking at new and potent geographies such as India or China. So it is imperative to start customising their offerings for these financially-significant markets. While ad-hoc efforts are made, there is no structured strategy in place to effectively tap these markets. The need of the hour is to develop a deeper understanding of the history and culture of these geographies.

A key element that makes a luxury brand work wonders is EMOD, or Every Moment Of Discipline. Every touch-point needs to be properly trained to handle clients. Customer experience is a key element that generates loyalty. A call centre executive or a store attendant can significantly contribute towards gaining a customer or losing him or her for good, generating good or bad publicity in the process. This is a critical area, especially in the age of social media.

From a brand's perspective, the most important golden rule is to keep your promise made to the customer. It is sacrosanct and under no circumstance can it be compromised, otherwise the integrity of the brand comes into question.

While luxury brands need to make their Richie Rich customers or "haves" feel exclusive and pampered, a close eye must be kept on the masses that keep the coffers filled. The sheer volume of masstige (a portmanteau of 'mass' and 'prestige' and has been described as 'prestige for the masses') sale helps every luxury brand worth its salt show the rosy numbers. While the big-ticket purchases are very important, the smaller-ticket buys make magic. So maintain a fine balance between the haves and the have-nots.

Finally, luxury branding is all about telling stories. The right mix of targeted marketing and communication of these brand stories create aspiration in the eyes of the customers.

Chapter 2

What's ailing the conventional 'Asia Strategy'

Luxury brands globally always make the mistake of having a so-called overall "Asia Strategy", which primarily involves two countries that are different in more ways than one. These two countries, India and China, have historically been very diverse in demonstrating their opulence and even today, they represent very different categories of luxury brand consumers. Let me elaborate with a bit of historical perspective.

Imagine a time when 20% of global sales of Rolls Royce used to come from India. During the early 1900s, the love Indian royalty had for branded luxury reached its pinnacle. Some examples of this are:

In 1926, the Maharaja of Patiala commissioned Cartier to remodel his crown jewels, which included a 234.69-carat De Beers diamond. The result was a breath-taking Patiala necklace adorned with 2,930 diamonds weighing 962.25 carats.

In 1928, the Maharaja of Jammu & Kashmir placed orders for 30 custom-made trunks from Louis Vuitton over a period of six months.

A certain Nizam had procured 50 Harley Davidsons for his postmen to deliver his messages.

India, as is evident from the examples above, has a rich legacy of using luxury since the inception of these international brands, unlike China. The prosperous community, even the royalty in China, have been closed and heavily dependent on exquisite local products. The pride of "made in China" to the wealthy locals was a Great Wall that barred the entry of foreign luxury brands.

In India, the scenario took a 180-degree turn post-Independence and anything remotely opulent was frowned upon. It's only in the past few decades that there has been a shift, and the 'New Maharajas' – industrialists, entrepreneurs, professionals and the rural rich – started blatantly adoring and flaunting all things luxurious.

Another very strong category of luxury consumers in India is the great Indian middle class. The monogrammed Louis Vuitton products might be reaching a New Maharaja's household time and again, but they also reach hundreds of households in the great aspiring middle class for the first time.

However, the Chinese market is not dominated by either of these above categories. The new-found growth in the luxury sector is fuelled only by the new, young, upper-middle class with a tendency to spend rather than save. They are the new-generation, first-time customers for luxury products. In China, the 'New Maharajas' are averse to 'foreign' luxury brands; the middle class is rising as a consumer, but has not been able to make a mark yet in the top lines of these brands.

Unfortunately, in spite of these marked differences, international luxury brands still find it convenient to have a common overall strategy for consumers in India and China. This a strategically wrong.

The approach of these luxury giants is very ad-hoc and clearly lacks a comprehensive and cohesive strategy. For example, you will suddenly see a slew of products launched to commemorate the Chinese New Year. Similar efforts will be made to cash in on celebrations like Diwali in India. There have been sporadic efforts too, like Hermes deciding to suddenly come up with an expensive saree, out of the blue.

If the strategic objective is to get a significant pie of the markets in China or India, or for that matter anywhere in the globe, the first thing these brands need to do is to understand the intrinsic nature of the consumers. The best way to know that is by customer immersion, understanding their traditions with a historical perspective.

It becomes easy to put together a comprehensive strategy towards creating an aspiration for the brand and converting these buyers as loyal customers once there is complete clarity on the evolution of the luxury consumer in a given geography.

It's time to wipe clean the overall 'Asia Strategy', and replace it with strategies for specific geographies with a deeper understanding of their traditions, culture and history.

Chapter 3

Search for perfect USP

USP or Unique Selling Proposition is the factor that makes a product or service "different" and "better" than that of their competitors. Theodore Levitt, a professor at Harvard Business School, said, "Differentiation is one of the most important strategic and tactical activities in which companies must constantly engage."

The issue is how can a brand custodian frame a proposition which is unique and will compel the customers to be loyal to your brand, or tempting as it sounds, switch their loyalty away from the competition?

USP is even more critical in luxury marketing because of the premium that these brands charge. It plays a key role in justifying the value for money for price-sensitive Indian customers. In luxury, the choice of USP becomes a critical exercise as there may even be a case when the strongest element of the brand may not necessarily be unique to it. So while the brand needs to strategically focus on its strength, it may have to focus on some other element for defining its USP.

Let us consider a watch brand. Its USP or core strength cannot be that it is Swiss-made. The competition has been exploiting it since time immemorial. Rolex, a watch with core strength of patented complications and movements can use this as far as its strategy charting is concerned. However, its USP can't be this patent because all its competitors have some movement or complication patented. Therefore, Rolex creates a USP with its campaign "Live for Greatness" using great leaders such as JFK and Martin Luther King Jr.

Another watch, which is priced way higher than Rolex, is Patek Phillippe. Unlike most be-jewelled high-end Rolex models, Patek Phillippe has a very traditional handcrafted design. Its USP, as stated in its most popular campaign, is "You never actually own a Patek Philippe. You merely look after it for the next generation." This beautiful campaign, primarily with father and son duos, established in the minds of customers that this watch deserves to be expensive as it transcends generations. Even in this case, Patek's core strength lies in its patented movements and complications.

The unique selling proposition creates differentiation in the minds of customers, making them prefer one brand over the other, irrespective of the fact that both of them are Swiss-made with patented movements and complications.

"There are journeys that turn into legends" was a very impactful "Core Values" campaign by Louis Vuitton where the brand was able to create its USP, keeping its competition far behind, with names like Sir Sean Connery. This USP conjures the image of icons using Louis Vuitton bags in their legendary journey, luring the customers into becoming a part of that imagery. The core strength, which will strategically be the key to LV, would, however, be something else – such as the quality of its canvas or its Damier signature design.

The unique selling proposition is also intricately related to another very critical concept for luxury brands – positioning. This refers to the space that a brand occupies in the customers' minds and how it is distinguished from the products of the competitors. Originally,

positioning focused on the product and with
Ries and Trout, grew to include building a
product's reputation and ranking among
competitor's products. USP is typically what
you think is your uniqueness for selling your
product or service, whereas positioning is what
your target audience thinks of you. So while a
brand needs to focus on its USP, it is imperative
that an outside-in approach is simultaneously
taken so as to understand what the audience
perceives as its differentiator. So, every brand
custodian has to consider both the inside-out as
well as outside-in approaches while crafting the
unique selling proposition for a luxury brand.

Chapter 4

Multi-billion-dollar wedding industry

In India, beside monsoon, the only season that is here to stay in that of weddings. And small wonder, amid the slew of celebrity marriages, the cacophony hit crescendo with the Ambani wedding. While the events were dripping wealth, there was a dominance of traditional Indian labels and non-labels, which exuded luxury by their sheer presence. Conspicuously missing were the international luxury labels, which have managed to become an integral part of the daily lives of these stakeholders, but remain somewhat amiss in one of the most important days of their lives – the big fat Indian wedding. So let's explore why these international luxury brands been so shy in getting a pie of this multi-billion-dollar wedding market in India?

First we have to identify the missing ingredient. And to know the missing ingredient, we have to understand the ethos of an Indian wedding. The root lies in our traditions. So what the wedding showcases is the celebration of the traditions in the most authentic way, making ample room to showcase opulence and luxe. Billions of dollars are mostly spent on non-international luxury brands to make sure that the heady mix of splurge and tradition is maintained.

The key lies in a deeper understanding of the Indian traditions and then customising the products to suit the occasion. Arrogance and pride for their craft and market have historically prevented international luxury brands from customisation for a certain geography. Much later, many of them realised business is more important than pride and so they started coming with customised collections which are geography-specific, especially for the two largest markets – India and China.

For example, to celebrate the Chinese Lunar New Year, Giorgio Armani's collection had dominance of the colour red, which symbolises good fortune and joy. It is used with this year's ubiquitous design element: dog. According to the Chinese zodiac calendar, 2018 was the Year of Dog. Christian Dior also released a dedicated video to introduce the exclusive "Rose des vents" jewellery collection. Louis Vuitton created a cartoon dog based on the Japanese Shiba Inu breed for this Lunar New Year.

On the Indian side, Diwali has been the most sought-after festival for these brands. A good example is a Spanish brand dedicated since 1953 to the creation of art porcelain figurines, Llardo. They came up with Lakshmi figurines and diyas made of porcelain for Diwali. Hermes had launched its saree for the Indian market, which had takers, but did not encourage the French luxury brand to come up with more. Jimmy Choo, too, has some collections dedicated to the Indian market. But they are destined for failure if they do not go deeper into understanding the traditions they are customising their collections for. For example, while both Diwali and Dhanteras are occasions for splurging and showcasing wealth, in the former, the buying is for gifting while in the latter, it is for within the family – preserving Lakshmi within the household. So the customisations will be very different if a luxury brand chooses to tap into these markets.

While luxury brands have taken a step towards acknowledging the importance of these markets, they are yet to acknowledge the criticality of greater understanding of the traditions and its ethos. Understanding the customers and what they intend to showcase via the various days of celebrations of the wedding is the key to the multi-billion-dollar Indian wedding industry. These brands need to take a closer look at the various rituals and then they will understand the customers' needs that they are not able to meet or satisfy currently – basically the need gap. Customer immersion is the only way by which they will be able to strategise and thus understand the range of products that they can come up with to be an integral part of the celebrations. Indianisation of international luxury brands is the only way they can get a pie of the wedding market.

There is, however, a catch. These international brands need to also keep in mind that the right mix is the only solution to success. In their zeal towards becoming Indian, they can't lose their essence, which is the raison d'être.

So, the right portion to the multi-billion-dollar magical potion is the magical mantra to be invited in the big, fat Indian wedding.

Chapter 5

Trick of making luxe worth your wait

We are such stuff

As dreams are made on; and our little life

Is rounded with a sleep.

  – William Shakespeare in *The Tempest*,
    Act 4, Scene 1

The immortal words by the bard capture the objective of any luxury brand. Luxury dazzles and weaving dreams with a touch of fantasy is what keeps the dazzle alive, ensuring the survival of a luxury brand.

The strategic aim of any luxury brand is to create aspirations. A neat trick that all the luxury brands play to keep the dreams going is that the product that they advertise the most is never available at their boutiques. Across the globe, they will make you wait while they keep fuelling your desire to own it by advertising it more and more.

A recent case is about Rolex GMT Master II, popularly known as 'Pepsi' because of its colour combination. This model was made popular by an American actor James Todd Spader in a series called Blacklist. After the official launch, the demand started to soar across all stores. So instead of producing more, Rolex decided that it will just keep increasing the waitlist. Two months back, I checked in Dubai Mall that the waiting time was four years. Hermes Birkin has been well known for an even longer waiting period. These brands believe the longer the waiting, the more the longing. The downside of it is that these brands also end up losing customers to competition because of unrealistic waiting periods.

These are the stuff dreams are made of, and so, when you actually have it, the dream is over. It is funny the way our minds work, especially of the Richie Rich (RR).

Another challenge these brands face is because of a certain characteristic of the consumer – relativity. Luxury is relative. What dazzles you may not dazzle me and definitely may not dazzle a Maharaja or, in today's parlance, the RR.

So while it is comparatively easy to weave a dream for me, it is pretty challenging to do the same for an RR who can easily get anything that money can buy. How can you create this El Dorado? This is where customisation plays a key role. While I may be enamoured by the sheer presence of a Rolls Royce Phantom, the RR, who already owns a few, will be equally enamoured with a Rolls Royce which has his or her initials and not of the Rolls Royce carved by the company on the bonnet in the same font and style. We frequently see cases wherein these companies love to customise their cars for these special customers by covering them with diamonds and rubies.

And last but not the least, another very effective strategy that luxury brands use to keep the dreams alive is by creating the "limited edition" myth. Let's give you a sneak peek into the minds of the RR when it comes to buying luxury goods. The fact that they can buy anything that has a price tag, is a double-edged sword cutting both ways. One, they are happy to know that they are people with means and so can afford almost anything in the realm of luxury brands. Second, because they can afford it, they are unhappy as there is no fun in it, no dream, no aspiration. The myth of limited edition comes to the rescue here. So even if the RR can afford such a luxury item, the dream is woven by money not being the decisive factor in possessing the same. So this makes the owner feel special, even compared with the other RRs as he or she is the proud owner of a limited edition.

The RR's mind works in strange ways and so the luxury brands have to keep innovating to keep the dreams alive and their cash registers ringing.

The Spirit of Ecstasy - Rolls Royce

II. Brand

Chapter 6

Images luxe conjures

What is the first thing that strikes you when you look at a luxury brand? What is the image a brand conjures in your mind? Is it a positive sentiment or negative? Is it inspiring or is it shameful? Does it make you long for it, make you yearn? Or it brings back a memory of a crime or scandal? For example, when you look at diamonds, do they bring thoughts of blood diamonds? So do you take an extra initiative to make sure the diamonds you are using are not bloody? This is where brand identity comes in.

When you come to know that the diamond is from De Beers or a Tiffany's, do you still have a doubt on its credibility? No, because these brands over the years have been able to establish their identity with clean diamonds. What the customer associates a brand's identity with makes all the difference. That perception alone can make or break a brand and it becomes an integral part of the brand identity. Not only are you confident that these brands do not use blood diamonds but you are also okay with paying a hefty premium for them. But do you have a mechanism by which you can be certain? No. However, it never matters as the perception war is already won.

Brand positioning is the key element when it comes to building perception in luxury. "The basic approach of positioning is not to create something new and different, but to manipulate what's already in the mind, to retie the connections that already exist," said Al Ries and Jack Trout in their book *Positioning: The battle for your mind*. Thus, it is all about how you are perceived in the eyes of the consumers and the art of manipulating that.

The idea of luxe is to dazzle and that dazzle essentially is perception. To me, a Rolls Royce Phantom exudes royalty and class. As I wrote in *Dark Luxe* on Phantom: "There is a saying that I run on reputation. I am the Phantom of reputation. I am the Rolls Royce Phantom. I am the mark of class, snobbery – the ultimate in luxury. When I drive down the road, people bow with respect and awe." However, to the Maharaja in that story, the same Rolls Royce Phantom was a mere collector of garbage. His perception is very different. The news that he has sent out a Phantom to collect garbage had spread like wildfire and had resulted in a steep fall in its sales in India. Just to put things in perspective, India market accounted for 25% global sales of Phantom in the 1920s. Perception made all the difference.

Let me give you another example. You see a socialite stepping out of a BMW carrying a Gucci clutch. You probably won't think that the clutch is a counterfeit. On the other hand, when another lady steps out of a radio taxi and is carrying the same clutch, a part in you screams that it has to be a fake. This is what perception is all about. The brand identity here is that if you are stepping out of a BMW, you are rich and affluent, and so can afford an expensive clutch. So for Gucci, the brand identity is that it is expensive, so people who can afford expensive cars can easily afford expensive bags, but that can't be said of people who are travelling in a taxi.

The irony is that it is quite possible that in the first case, the clutch could be a fake, and in the second, a genuine one. The rich and the affluent often take resort to expensive first copies as they have to visit many parties every day and cannot afford to repeat their dress or stilettoes or clutch. Thus, first copies come to the rescue. And as they are aware of the popular perception, they know no one will doubt whether their clutch or stilettoes are genuine as long as they are stepping out of a BMW.

It is all a matter of creating the right identity by manipulating perception.

Chapter 7

Controversy, thy name is luxe

First let us understand the Chinese luxury consumers and market, which recently came into the news for boycotting Italian luxury brand Dolce & Gabbana (D&G) over alleged racist remarks.

According to a recent study, by 2025, the value of the global luxury goods market will climb to around $450 billion and 7.6 million Chinese households will represent $150 billion of that pie, an amount equivalent to the combined size of the US, the UK, French, Italian and Japanese markets in 2016. Chinese consumers will account for 44% of the total global market by 2025.

So it is natural that all the luxury giants have their eyes on China. They have all started customising collections based on important events such as the Chinese New Year to showcase how important China is for them.

For Dolce & Gabbana too, the "Shanghai Great Show" was a step in that direction, in line with their strategy to capture this pie. But alas, it backfired. This Italian fashion house had to cancel this major show after controversial videos and offensive private Instagram messages, allegedly sent by co-founder Stefano Gabbana, went viral on social media. Celebrities and models in China deserted the brand immediately. The designer has, however, denied writing the messages, stating his Instagram account was hacked.

It all began with a promotional video featuring an Asian model in a red D&G dress, trying to use chopsticks to eat pizza, spaghetti and a giant version of the Italian pastry cannoli. A series of direct messages on Instagram went viral where Gabbana complains about criticisms of the video. The Italian designer is then accused of making derogatory remarks directed towards China and the Chinese people as he defends the ads. This resulted in a mass boycott in China, even after Gabbana's apology and a cry that his account was hacked.

Another example of such controversial remarks is by champagne brand Cristal. It was the delight of billionaire rapper Jay-Z and he had used it in his music videos, resulting in huge publicity. Unfortunately, the high was short-lived for the brand. *The Economist* interviewed Frederic Rouzaud, the then managing director of Cristal, in 2006 and he was asked how the owners felt about seeing rappers sip their gold in their music videos. "That's a good question," he replied, with a biting follow-up: "But what can we do? We can't forbid people from buying it. I'm sure Dom Perignon or Krug would be delighted to have their business." Jay-Z was appalled and the brand suffered the brunt of their racist views.

Almost a decade ago, founder of another well-known fashion brand Tommy Hilfiger faced the storm when he allegedly said that doesn't want minorities wearing his clothes.

And then there is the controversial history of brands and their associations such as the story of Hugo Boss joining the Nazi party in 1931. The all-black SS uniform was produced by the Hugo Boss company, along with the brown SA shirts and the uniforms of the Hitler Youth. Some of his factory workers during this period were also French and Polish prisoners of war who were forced into labour.

These controversies have in almost all cases impacted the top-line and bottom-line of these luxury brands adversely and has also eroded the brand value to an extent that buyers decided not to be associated with them. These brands end up becoming a social stigma, an outcast in the respective impacted geographies among its hitherto-loyal clienteles. The need of the hour is a sensitisation drive among all luxury brands – from the owners to the ground attendants who directly handle customers every day. While these luxury majors clearly understand the economic importance of certain geographies such as China and India, they fail to give any serious heed to their culture and history.

Chapter 8

Karl and the art of brand legacy

The passing away of iconic fashion designer Karl Lagerfeld gave rise to a very important question – What will happen to his brand now? Which makes us think, how to create a brand legacy?

Will a customer still have the same unshakable faith in the brand when the icon is no longer running the show? When customers become loyal to a brand, especially a renowned one like Karl Lagerfeld, they do not buy it for the design or style or aesthetics or flaunt quotient alone. The personality of the icon becomes the X-factor, which demands the premium as well as the loyalty. So when that icon is no longer there, the loyalty of the customers is bound to take a hit. In art, the creativity of the artist is captured on canvas and thus after the artist is gone, the prices soar. In fashion, once the icon is gone, there may be a sudden surge resulting from emotional buying by customers, but it is bound to fall soon.

Karl Lagerfeld was the creative director for two iconic brands – Chanel and Fendi. However, the dent these two fashion houses will suffer will be significantly less compared with the legendary designer's own fashion house. Chanel and Fendi, unlike his own brand, are no longer represented by faces or personalities.

Apple's situation after the death of Steve Jobs comes close to this issue that ails Lagerfeld's fashion house. While a lot of persona was attached to the products and Jobs was the face of Apple, the company was still able to move on after a brief setback, and one critical reason was the name – Apple, not Jobs.

Louis Vuitton did not face this danger when their creative designer Marc Jacobs moved on and started his own label. Gucci carried on successfully after Tom Ford left. But what if Tom Ford or Marc Jacobs decided to take a break from their own brands?

This leads to a Catch 22 situation. You can't gain complete trust of the customers without giving a face to the brand. On the other hand, if there's a prominent face to a brand, what happens when the face is not there anymore? What should be the right portion of persona that a brand creator needs to put in to leave a legacy? Here are five golden rules:

1. The brand needs to create a perception that it is professionally run. This plays a key role in ensuring that while there is a face, the brand is run by professionals. Even after the death of Coco Chanel, the brand's legacy not only lived on, but also kept growing. The brand of Alexander McQueen, on the other hand, faced a tough time after his untimely death. Apple, too, had a slight setback before it bounced back.

2. Faceless brands such as Rolex and Louis Vuitton thus have an edge. These brands are more affected by the demand cycles, not the presence or absence of personalities. These brands, however, have created a persona of their own, based on their style quotient. They have successfully used icons as brand ambassadors to give their brands a face, a persona and a legacy.

3. The billion-dollar questions for a brand creator are – when should he or she pour his or her personality into the brand and when should the brand start developing its own persona? While establishing the brand should always be the primary responsibility, it is also important to give professionals a free hand to run the

machinery. The creator should focus on the creative side of the business.

4. The key lies in succession planning. A brand creator needs to wake up to the thought of planning for a successor who will keep the legacy on. It is best if this successor gets some handholding from the creator so that he or she can imbibe the key elements of the brand personality, so that loyal customers do not feel cheated.

5. It is the brand promise that makes it powerful. So the most important element for a brand to create a legacy is to keep its promises. This will help them create a history.

Chapter 9

A fake, is a fake, is a fake.

Why does a consumer spend hard-earned money, and that too willingly, on something that is not authentic? What can be the lure to buy a fake, a counterfeit? How can luxury brands make sensible people so blind that they make a beeline outside offline or online stores for getting their hands on these counterfeits?

Let me give you some salient pointers on luxury counterfeits:

- Growing at a breakneck speed of 40-45%, the luxury counterfeit market touched $1 billion-mark in 2018.

- There are grades of these luxury counterfeit products and the best ones are called first copy. They are distinctly different from the so-called cheaper versions of fakes that are easily available online or offline.

- The two most counterfeited brands are Rolex and Louis Vuitton.

- Some e-commerce sites sell counterfeits declaring them as authentic, at unbelievable discounts. The photographs used in all such cases are illegally taken from the official websites of the luxury brand so as to create this myth of authenticity.

- There has been a surge in the growth of the counterfeit market with the onset of e-commerce. While earlier these fakes were bought secretly in blind alleys, now they can be shopped from your mobile and delivered at home, at your convenience.

- There are some distinct identifiers for all luxury brand goods that help sieve the fakes.

Now let me delve a little deeper into this curious case of first copies. If you look at a fake Rolex Datejust or Day Date, there will be marked differences that even an untrained eye will be able to spot. But for a first copy, only expert eyes will be able to spot the differences. For example, a first copy watch will have high-quality steel, sapphire crystal case and precise mechanical movement like the original. The master watchmaker has not only replicated the complication with precision, but also kept an eye on the identifiers. In my book *Dark Luxe,* I have shared the story of Master W who has been passing on this talent of fine watchmaking over generations. Now, unfortunately, he has to make first copies, but he does it with the same dedication and pride.

For the past few years, in my quest for understanding luxe, I have been exploring and researching the counterfeit markets in Europe, Middle East, Southeast Asia and India. Speaking extensively to the sellers as well as buyers across these markets, I have gathered that there is a huge demand for luxury fakes, as they are cheap. Also, the demand for first copies is low across these markets as most consumers, according to these sellers, do not understand the difference and thus can't justify the price differential.

But why buy a fake? The blame falls squarely on the brand built by these luxury goods. They create an aspiration among the so-called 'have-nots' to own, rather possess these labels, these logos. It gives a sense of entitlement, most buyers said. And they assume that the people they are going to flaunt these labels to also will not be able to figure out whether it is a fake or an authentic. Thus, the objective is to showcase, rather flaunt, to others one's entitlement and purchasing power. And thus, the rise and rise of the counterfeit market.

Counterfeits also give rise to democratization of luxury. Even the 'have-nots' can now flaunt the labels of the 'haves', albeit the counterfeits, that the former only could aspire for earlier. Even luxury brands are exploiting this sentiment with their masstige category.

What is curious about the first copy luxury product is that primary consumers are not the 'have-nots', but the 'haves'. This is a category which is a heavy consumer of luxury brands and prefers some first copies on the side. For example, a friend of mine told me that she has to go to three-four parties every night and she can't repeat the brands of her clutch or her stilettos. Thus, she has decided to mix and match originals and first copies, all for the eyes of the beholder.

However, a fake is a fake is a fake!

Chapter 10

Ruling the logo land

Imagine an ice cube or a cookie branded by a luxury brand such as Louis Vuitton or Gucci. Luxury has surely made inroads into areas earlier never fathomed. So is that designer cookie more delectable? Apparently, yes. Thanks to the power of the logo.

In my second book of the Luxe trilogy, *Dark Luxe*, I have written about the power of logo and how it acts as a seductress to the flaunters, whose primary area of appreciation is the logo of luxury brands that they can flaunt. So, to them, more than the craftsmanship or legacy of the brand, it is the logo that matters. They pay for the label. The logo needs to have a flaunt quotient, and be rest assured, they will keep loving it.

The power of the logo has its pros as well as cons. Let me deal with the pros first.

Brand awareness: One of the biggest advantages of a well-recognised logo is in creating brand awareness among the customers.

Once a brand custodian is able to create an aspirational quotient with their products, it is the logo that furthers that craving with the customers. Whenever a customer sees the logo, there will be an increased need for owning it. This aspiration impacts all the customer categories but is most dominant among flaunters, who will flock to the nearest boutiques to get their hands on this desirable logo. For these customers, what they are buy will not matter much. It can be a bag, a dress, shoes, or accessories such as a coin purse or sunglasses. Their purchases are never need-based but based on the desire to flaunt the new logo in the town.

Counters ringing: The flaunters also contribute significantly to the sale of masstige products. Masstige is all about the logo. They benefit the most from the increased desirability of the logo. So it contributes to the sheer volume of luxury consumption.

Now let us look at the negatives.

Counterfeits: The more desirous the logo, the more desperation it creates among consumers. If you are not happy with masstige products, the counterfeit e-bazaar is just a click away. No wonder, the most counterfeited logos are Louis Vuitton and Rolex. Growing at a compounded annual growth rate of almost 40-45%, the counterfeit luxury products market in India is likely to more than double to Rs 5,600 crore by 2022 from the current level of about Rs 2,500 crore. A reason why the market of luxury fakes is growing at such a fast pace is the advent of e-commerce platforms selling the goods at lucrative prices. Web shopping portals account for over 25% of the fake luxury goods market in India.

Business loss (notional): One has to understand that flaunters not always belong to the great Indian middle class, but can be Richie Rich as well. But instead of big-ticket purchases, they will go for a token purchase just to own the brand. This leads to notional business loss. So, for example, instead of buying a Louis Vuitton trunk, a flaunter ends up buying a coin purse.

To conclude, even with all the shortfalls, one can never deny the sheer power of the logos. Luxe dazzles its customers and owning the logo creates a sense of belonging in them, which makes them feel special, as desirable as the logos.

So for luxury brands, it is all about ruling the logo land.

Chapter 11

The times they a changin'

In remote Yamunanagar, a farmer gifts his only son a pristine white BMW 3 Series on his twenty-first birthday. The son immediately takes the brand new 'ultimate driving machine' for a spin. The son, Akash, then takes the car close to the river and finally, lo and behold, he drives it overboard! Locals said that he jumped out of the vehicle just before it reached deeper water and onlookers helped him to safety. Reason? He wanted a Jaguar XF and BMW was "too small" for him and his friends. The boy's father told the media, "I wanted to give my son a birthday present. We could only afford to give him a BMW, while he kept on insisting that he be given a Jaguar. He said the vehicle was too small, but we thought he'd be okay with the BMW."

Now this stray incident took place in a remote Haryana village. The video of the drowning car not only became viral in India, but also made it to international news channels like Fox News, which very smartly embedded ads of Jaguar's latest models in the news.

In today's global village, crisis can come from any quarter. For any luxury brand, this category is a typical buyer community that thrives on "ego" and "flaunt quotient". They are cash rich and their basis of selection of brand is typically their perception of the extent to which it will give them a higher status within their community. So if they think Jaguar is the aspiration and BMW is "too small", so much so that it should be thrown away into the river, this is a big jolt to brand equity of the latter and a huge boost for the former. I will not be surprised if Jaguar sales rise in that belt and BMW's plummet.

So such stray incidents need immediate crisis management. Every luxury brand knows that their forte lies is creating a perception and managing it. A luxury product is like a ticket to a dream world conjured by brand custodians. As long the dream is alive, the perception is alive as well. That way, then, the brand keeps thriving and charging a premium.

With the onset of digital media, crisis management has become a very tough task, as the speed of news has become real time. And crisis can now hit the company from any geography. So perception management as well as brand equity management has become a real time job. No longer can a brand afford to wait for a day to prepare a media release. Gone are those days. Long gone. In today's day and age, it is all about reaching out to the potential and existing customers in real time.

There are two thumb rules:

1. Start firefighting in the same medium where the crisis has erupted. If the crisis has erupted on Twitter, the brand can't afford to target print media journalists or editors.

2. Keep a close eye on the noise in digital media. This will help a brand custodian to sense a brewing concern and address the issue before it snowballs into a crisis.

Little did Akash know or realise the harm he has done to a world class automobile brand like BMW. But his peers, friends, will be quick in spreading the word far and wide in the buyer community that "BMW is too small". Such a crisis needs focused campaigns in target areas. One thought can be on how "spacious" and "comfortable" BMW is, beside the riding pleasure and the luxury quotient. Just to override the "too small" notion.

So in this world rendered too small by technology, an "arrogant" youth in Yamunanagar can give sleepless nights to an auto giant headquartered in Munich.

The Equestrian Knight - **Burberry**

III. Perception

Chapter 12

Musings of millennial millionaires

Did Rolex ever fathom their biggest competition will be a technology giant – Apple. Smartwatches by Cupertino, a California-based company have become the biggest threat to the legendary Swiss watchmaker.

And lo and behold, they have even come up with solid gold versions to bring the price range in direct competition to Rolex. It is the best of technology and luxe on your wrist.

How times are changing! When the pace and preferences of tech-tuned, temperamental millennials are forcing businesses to be on tenterhooks, can luxury behemoths ignore this dynamic generation?

There is an entirely new category of customers that are added to the existing classification of Experientialists, Connoisseurs, Flaunters and Aesthetes – make way for the millennial millionaires!

It is an entirely new category of buyers with a very different perception of luxury. These are the second or third generation Richie Rich with a spending capacity similar to affluent Baby boomers or Generation X.

Luxe custodians need to now pay close attention to the musings of these millennial millionaires.

The biggest challenge is that their worldview is not the same as their fathers' or grandfathers'. No wonder, Rolex is losing millions of potential customers to Apple. So how can luxury brands woo this new set of trailblazing consumers?

Decoding millennial millionaires: All luxury brands need to do a deep dive into the lives of these millennials to understand their choices and preferences. The objective of this customer immersion is to understand a very fundamental question – what dazzles them? 'Old wine in a new bottle' strategy will work for them. What has historically worked, will work no more. Some characteristics of these millennial millionaires are:

- In today's connected world, they know the latest trends in luxury, fashion and technology across the globe.
- They are impatient, so they need to be convinced very quickly.

- They are very demanding customers and will always want their preferred product yesterday. So they need to be handled with care.
- They are impulsive buyers, so all brands need to have a deep understanding of using this impulse for their benefit, especially in their marketing strategy.
- They will not bat an eyelid before changing their preferred brand. So never take brand loyalty for granted.
- Luxury brands have to bring in a "cool" quotient to woo them. Traditional excellence will not work well.

Preference for digital media: This generation lives with latest technology and mostly in a virtual world. This is a boon and a bane for luxe. Earlier, there was a huge issue of suitable and prime real estate for these luxury brands to set shop. These needed to be in the crème-de-la-crème locations to woo the so-called New Maharajas and give them a royal experience. But getting such real estate was becoming a huge problem, both in terms of availability and cost, for all these brands across the globe. Today, with the advent of e-marketplaces, this problem is resolved. So millennials prefer their luxury shopping online, and not offline. Ironically, solutions often come with problems. E-commerce has given an enormous boost to the counterfeit industry wherein hundreds of new websites have popped up, showcasing pics of original luxury goods being sold at heavy discounts of up to 80%. Most millennials are not even aware that they are buying fakes.

New-age ads: Marketing luxury has always been a challenge as the objective always is to create a sense of aspiration and exclusivity. Inspiring personalities who have created a legacy were the first choices as brand ambassadors or representatives of the brands, such as JFK for Rolex. Niche magazines were identified wherein advertisements were given. These two very potent ways of advertising fall flat as far as these millionaire millennials are concerned. Therefore, new models need to be identified – personalities who are "cool" and "inspiring". The choice of advertising media also needs to be changed to include a heavy dose of digital and social media. The millennials prefer videos to print ads and their attention span is reduced to seconds. Therefore, all luxury marketers have to invest in new-age campaigns through the right media with loads of "cool" quotient to woo these millennial millionaires. Instagram and Snapchat are more relevant than a Forbes or a Fortune.

Tech Talk: This by far is the biggest threat. As stated earlier, the way Apple is eating into Rolex's market, all luxury brands need to be careful from not only their immediate competitors, but also these tech companies. These millennial millionaires swear by technology, and thus, the latest in technology carries the most "cool" quotient. All luxury brands need to keep an eye on the latest technology trends and products that lure these millennials, and shape their strategy accordingly.

Chapter 13

Masstige – Luxury of the Masses

The essence of a luxury brand lies in the exclusivity it offers. While this exclusivity subtly opens its doors to moolah, unfortunately, it does not necessarily keep counters ringing for all.

Thus, as a survival strategy, all luxury brands owe their existence to a very special category – the masstige. A portmanteau of the words 'mass' and 'prestige', 'masstige' has been described as 'prestige for the masses'. The term was popularised by Michael Silverstein and Neil Fiske in their book *Trading Up* and a Harvard Business Review article titled 'Luxury for the Masses'.

Masstige products are defined as "premium but attainable," and have two aspects: (1) They are considered luxury or premium products, and (2) They have price points that fill the gap between mid-market and super premium.

Luxury has indeed become a volume game with the great Indian middle class, leading the luxe game from the front.

Let's take the example of Louis Vuitton's Speedy 30 handbag, which has been nicknamed the three-second bag in Korea because it feels like you see one every three seconds. As one of the many entry-level products, this has been developed to deliver value for money on a smaller, yet perhaps equally indulgent taste of the brand narrative. So, entry-level products – accessories, belts, scarves, wallets, small purses, and the likes – of the luxury brands have a clear demand among this segment. They cater to the need of just flaunting the labels.

While exclusivity remains the key element, all luxury brands extend downwards with these low-hanging, seemingly-affordable fruits to whet the appetite of the value-for-label masses. Today, masstige products have democratised luxury and made it accessible to both the *raja* (the king) and the *praja* (the subjects) alike.

Another key advantage of masstige is that it keeps counterfeits and first copies at bay. The members of the great Indian middle class are logo-conscious and yet feel a little pang when they have to shell out a bomb to flaunt a luxury brand. At the same time, they also feel guilty when they choose to use luxury counterfeits for satiating their need to flaunt luxury. However, thanks to the masstige products, this multi-billion dollar counterfeit market takes a hit. With scarfs, belts, coin purses, perfumes of the luxury brands being available at prices, which to the price-sensitive Indian buyers are worth the logo, they end up moving away from buying counterfeits and first copies.

But, what if this greed for the bottomline from masstige steals the luxury brand's exclusivity quotient? To what extent can the brand be diluted without taking a hit? In my book *Decoding Luxe* I have formulated a three-part solution on how luxury brands can get the right mix of their products, without diluting the brand and keeping the moolah flowing:

1. A brand needs to identify its signature products and add a premium to the prices. These are meant to tease the aspirations of the GIMC, who can't afford them. Mostly display the pictures of these signature items, making sure they are always out of stock, with fresh stock on

the anvil from Germany or France. The GIMC is sure to keep coming back.

2. A brand needs to identify special edition, handcrafted pieces that it wants the Richie Rich to buy. These should be on display so that the Richie Rich can get a feel of the product, and then take it home, just a like a piece of history. These have a premium attached due to their exclusivity.

3. And finally comes the masstige products to satiate the appetite of the GIMC for them to flaunt that logo of the brand they always aspired to buy.

Chapter 14

Of Flaunters and Bling Economy

For luxury brands, all that glitters is gold. Bling is a tried and tested strategy to attain glittering success.

To understand this better, let me first take you through the mindset of luxury consumers. As stated earlier, there are four categories in which I have classified luxury buyers globally in my book *Decoding Luxe*. They are Experientialists, Connoisseurs, Aesthetes and Flaunters.

Flaunters tend to value brand name over all other factors. Purchase of a brand is a symbol of their status in society. So the visibility of the brand name is important. It is also important for the brand to be aspirational, otherwise, what's the big deal? Badge seekers are mostly the neo-rich and young, having a strong desire to prove to the society that they have jumped aboard the elitist, luxury brand-wagon. They are driving luxury in India. And this is the category of logo seekers and flaunters to whom the bling appeals the most.

There are distinctly two categories of luxury brands – One goes all out to scream the bling; the other stays muted in its appeal to be classy. Let me elaborate a bit.

Consider Louis Vuitton. The brand has since inception believed in being the flaunter's favourite. If you look at old Bond movies, from luggage to briefcase to cheque-book covers to files, every leather accessory will carry the LV monogram. LV is historically designed in such a way that the brand is evident from a distance. A similar brand philosophy is with Rolex. The bling is an integral part of its brand philosophy.

No wonder, the two most trusted brands for the flaunters, including the debonair British spy James Bond, since time immemorial have been Louis Vuitton and Rolex.

On the other extreme lie brands that prefer to be muted in their bling quotient as they prefer to attract the categories of connoisseurs and aesthetes, and not the flaunters. Examples are Montblanc and Bottega Veneta. While the former decided to be muted as writing instruments are meant to exude a sense of dignity and class, the latter's motto is "when your own initials are enough". So rather than having a logo, Bottega Veneta chose to celebrate Brand "you". In a way, even Rolls Royce has a similar sentiment; RR logo is enough and does not cater to the flaunter category. I am not considering the diamond-studded, solid gold, custom-made ones. For these brands, it is all about class, which the bling takes away.

And then with time, these classy brands realised that the demographic of the customers is shifting from 40-plus to 20-plus. Hip-hop stars who epitomise the bling in luxury are becoming icons and driving their sales. So Rolls Royce tried to take on blingy and flashy Ferrari by entering sports car segment; Montblanc launched a new collection with "MB" monogram, and so on.

The world of luxury is slowly and steadily getting caught in the bling economy.

Chapter 15

Art of Subliminal Marketing

Getting loud and on the face is the primary mantra for luxury branding. However, there is a relatively small, albeit growing and loyal segment which still believes in a subliminal appeal of luxury. Branding to them is very difficult and thus, an art. They loathe brands which do not have class and go all out to showcase their products in the most brazen way. They loathe the brands which are popular with customers who are flaunters. 'Money can't buy you class', that is the moot point that drives this genre of customers. For a better understanding of subtle and subliminal branding, let us first understand the buyer categories that need to be lured in – Connoisseurs and Aesthetes.

Let's first meet the Connoisseurs. This genre is passionate in certain areas of interest and makes it a point to be well-informed and knowledgeable about it. These categories could be art, scotch, wine, watches, writing instruments, cigars, horses, and the likes. These connoisseurs get together and appreciate the finer aspects of their passion. They look down upon people who do not share their passion. They form clubs and get together for a quiet appreciation of luxury of creation. It may be a horology society or a wine club or a scotch club or a cigar group. Being rich is a necessary but certainly not the sufficient condition for being a part of this exclusive group of connoisseurs. You need to belong to a certain class to be a part of this group.

They will spend their time and money in pursuit of the collection of personal passion points. They make the pursuit of their area of passion a mission and pursue it with zest. When it comes to limited editions, or handcrafted editions or spirit of the bygone era, these connoisseurs will not bat an eyelid before spending a fortune.

And then come the Aesthetes. To this genre, the brand is much less important than the design. Aesthetes are luxury consumers purely because they have arrived at a state of income due to which they can indulge in their love for design among luxury brands or products. They will shell out a bomb because the object of desire is hand-stitched and not because of the label. They pride themselves for having an eye that picks out the unique and bold in design. Again money or the brazen display of affluence is frowned upon by this category of buyers. They are more into the appreciation of finer things in life, and money surely can't develop that faculty.

The difference between them and the connoisseur is that the latter has certain passions which they follow with zeal and the quality and craftsmanship are very important. However, for the former category, it is the aesthetic appeal, the look, the intricacies of the design that appeal to their senses. They are also likely to pursue this aesthetic across categories, unlike a connoisseur.

Thus comes the art of subliminal marketing, which is the key for engaging both these customer categories. Brands need to focus on the story, the creativity and the uniqueness of a product and certainly not on the price point. It is very difficult to lure these two categories with the usual razzle dazzle that works for the majority of customers. On the contrary, bling drives these customers away from a brand. They are a serious lot, who has the potential of being loyal as well as brand ambassadors, spreading the good word. The key to make these two categories loosen their purse strings is to be subliminal and low key.

These customers usually come from old money and thus are not dazzled by luxury or rather price tags. They look for something unique in the product, so the branding has to be specific to showcasing the uniqueness of it. The brand story has to be told in a manner that attracts the interest of these Connoisseurs and Aesthetes. Be it the uniqueness of the design or the man hours spent by a master craftsman or the rarity of the raw material, the brand story has to appeal at a subliminal level.

For example, a rare brand of shawl Shahtoosh, meaning King of Wools, is now a banned item. It uses the wool from a rare Tibetan antelope. Master artisans weaved delicate hair, which measured between 7 and 10 microns, to make these shawls so fine that they can be passed through a wedding ring. The mere collection of wools from these migratory animals moving down from Mongolia to Tibet takes years. The branding of Shahtoosh, thus will have to be on

the rarity and not on the price tag to appeal at a
subliminal level.

Chapter 16

Darkness behind the veil of luxury

Luxury has always been for the chosen few, exclusive. Luxury creates a great divide between the haves and have-nots. You either have it or you don't; or rather, you can either afford it, or you can't. Luxury has its origin in the word luxe, which means dazzle. So, whenever you think of luxury, it is always about razzle-dazzle, it is always about glam and glitz. The stuff dreams are made of. Dreams that only the chosen few can buy. And every bit of luxury exudes a shine that blinds the have-nots. Sorry Mr Marx, this is not the world of the Proletariats.

Behind this razzle-dazzle, there is another life… A life as real as that of the have-nots… a life filled with lust, hatred, jealousy, anger… a life very deprived, very starved… a life of horrors… a life of flesh and blood… But yes, a life to die for, or rather kill!

Luxury remains a silent witness to that darkness.

This is a side that existed since the genesis of luxe, just like the dark side of the moon.

Luxury's dazzle paves way for the deadly sins and ego, which soon tear apart every moral fabric. In the core of luxe lies a sense of exclusivity, entitlement and this makes you feel above the cattle class, above the have-nots.

The darkness that hides behind the dazzle of luxury mostly remains secret; some even become folklore – either of royalty or corporate.

Let me share a folklore of a certain Maharaja who was snubbed by a Brit salesman in London at a Rolls-Royce store as he failed to recognise him and treated the Maharaja as an ordinary poor Indian. The Maharaja was shown the door. The Maharaja could not take the insult and returned the next day in his royal attire and bought all the six Phantoms, to be shipped to his kingdom. His ego was so hurt that just buying all the Phantoms in the showroom was not enough to soothe it. Once the Phantoms reached his kingdom, he ordered that they need to be decorated befitting their royalty. And then, he ordered these Phantoms to be used for collecting garbage, day after day. Rolls-Royce Phantom is a car that proverbially "runs on reputation", so the news spread like wildfire and caused a large dent in the revenues of the luxury car maker. The reputation was at stake. The Maharaja's ego was finally soothed. In one story in my book *Dark Luxe*, I have taken a creative liberty giving a Phantom a mind of its own, creating a 'what if' moment on revenge for reputation.

Then there are folklores of certain priceless gems that were responsible for writing the history of empires in blood.

Coming to a more known ground and its lesser-known darkness – the corporate tales of blood and gore. Espionage is a very common phenomenon, and luxury and fashion houses are no stranger to it. There are horror stories of usurping designs and ideas by rival houses, and then going to extents that will make even Dante contemplate a new Inferno. Last year, a headline hit the fashion world with French fashion house Saint Laurent Paris (YSL) being accused of copying a design of a clutch bag in Fall 2017 runway show at Paris Fashion Week. It was alleged to be a mirror image of the Mburu bag designed by Senegalese brand, Tongoro collection, launched by Sarah Diouf.

Earlier this year, this paper reported a story of a Delhi-based brand, People Tree, making allegations against Christian Dior after seeing their block prints on the cover of a magazine. "Featuring on the cover of *Elle* magazine, Sonam Kapoor was seen adorned in a boho-chic dress with the controversial print. The vibrant dress in the rustic shade was paired with a frilled multi-coloured patchwork shrug. While initially, it garnered a positive response, later on, allegations of 'blatant plagiarism' made the dress and its designer, Christian Dior, an internet buzz."

Luxury remains a constant lure, giving people a justification to go deep into the bottomless pits of hell. All these stories are guarded with life. But some spill over into nasty legal battles.

With the steady rise of consumerism, it is only fair to assume that luxe will remain the strongest lure for both the haves and have-nots, either the desire to remain exclusive or the desire to become one, and thus both can be pushed to the dark side.

Chapter 17

Of aspirations and mind games

What lies at the core of luxe is a deep desire. What drives luxe is again a deep desire. In the course of branding or marketing luxury, what we actually do is brand and market desire. Desire, however, is tricky. Because just like a human heart, it can swing both ways, taking luxe along with it, to both extremes. So like the age-old cassettes, there are two sides of it – Side A and Side B.

Side A: This one will be the positive side, which leads to aspirations. This is the side that keeps the fire of aspirations burning in the human hearts and thus counters ringing for luxury brands. This is the desire that keeps you awake at nights and makes you chase your dreams of dazzle.

Imagine this, you love fast cars and finally have stretched your budget to acquire your dream car - a BMW Z4. You have fulfilled your desire to drive the meanest machine in town. While driving your brand new dream car, say on the fifth day, suddenly, a Ferrari 812 Superfast zips past you. As a car enthusiast, you are well aware of the model and you know it is priced way beyond your budget, even in foreseeable future, at over five crore rupees. And you are a practical woman. Till the time you had only seen its photograph and it was fine to go for Z4. But the moment you see it in front of your eyes, something changed. In no time, you realise that your desire has a sudden change of heart. The Z4 has been removed from the throne of your dream car and replaced by 812 Superfast. You save a photograph of your new dream car on your phone, so that you can inspire yourself every day to own this new machine… as soon as possible.

In this way, desire helps you rise the ladder of luxury and so brand custodians or dream merchants are very quick to manipulate your desires so that they can achieve their targets. You need to understand that the dream merchants, while selling you the dream car, will make sure that there is a practical picture painted, so that in the quest of upgrading directly to 812 Superfast, you don't skip the intermediate step and not buy the Z4. They will make sure that they make you desire for both and also desire an upgrade immediately after you make the purchase. Thus, desires in the positive form of aspirations fuel the luxury industry.

Side B: Desire can also swing towards bottomless pits of hell and take luxury along with it. In my second book of the Luxe Trilogy, *Dark Luxe*, I have explored in details the second aspect of desire. This is the story of nightmares, about those realities that safely hide behind the veil of luxe. These are tales of fiction from the darkest pits of hell.

There are examples from life where luxury is made an accomplice to achieve the deepest and darkest desires. These are not aspirations, these are manifestations of the seven deadly sins and how desire makes luxe an integral part of it.

Let me elaborate with a story from *Dark Luxe*. This is a story of a golden pair of scissors which the younger brother uses to kill the Maharaja so that he can take over the throne. The significance of this pair is that these are the sharpest pair made of pure gold and was historically used to severe the placenta, separating a new born royal from the mother.

The caveat is that this ritual is meant only for the first born, the one who is entitled to the throne. Sheer jealousy and desire for the throne made the brother kill his brother with the same pair of scissors, which had given him his identity as the heir to the throne. Desire creates the darkest secrets, safely hidden in the corridors of power and luxury, and stays silent as a witness. Thus, branding desire is the elixir that a dream merchant aims to capture to brand the ultimate luxe.

Chapter 18

Discovering facets of Luxe Identity

What's an identity? May be our name, our gender, our profession, our family, things that define us. Isn't it? If we look at it spiritually, even these are not your identity; it is much deeper, known as your "original face" which you can only see once you go beyond these elements that you think define you.

A luxe brand also has an identity. It also has a gender, a family, and other elements that define it. Gender? Yes, let me explain. When you think of Rolex, is it historically a male brand. If you trace its historic advertising campaigns and brand ambassadors such as "Live for Greatness", which features JFK and Martin Luther King Jr. The brand is essentially an extension of the male identity.

An exclusive watch brand Patek Phillipe has an iconic ad campaign that recently completed twenty years, "You never actually own a Patek Philippe. You merely look after it for the next generation." A Patek watch isn't a device for telling time. It's an heirloom that transfers values across generations. Now if you closely look at the visuals, they are a father-son duo. It is only after much criticism of their gender bias that they decided to come up with a visual with a girl and her mother. But essentially, they focused singularly on the male identity of the watch.

There are two aspects of identity, just like our life. One is internal, what a brand thinks or oneself and the other is external, what consumers think of the brand.

The external identity becomes the real identity that matters at the end of the day. For example, a Patek can charge $2,500,000 for a timepiece. Now internally, it may think that this price is justified, given the identity of Patek as an heirloom. Now in commerce, this identity will not matter. The identity that will matter is what its consumers think it is really worth. So if there are no buyers at this price, then Patek's internal brand identity is not in line with the ground reality. Thus it warrants a serious course correction, which means a relook at the areas where the company needs to wake up and smell the coffee, thus to strategize how it can elevate the external identity to the aspired level.

And always, the market acts as a great leveller and is quick to tell a brand what it is actually worth. Then the brand needs to look into various facets to figure the way forward. A brand can choose one of the three strategies:

1. The brand stays arrogant and ignores the market signal completely.

2. The brand bows to the market pressure and revisits its pricing and corrects it.

3. The brand internally is confident of its worth and thus knows that the price is right, but it is not arrogant and respects the market. So it understands that the need of the hour is to strategize towards making the brand's external identity more exquisite.

While the first group loses the battle in no time, the second group is smart and wins the short-term battle. The third group, however, is the prudent one which wins the long-term battle. Market indicators are like an "acid test" for the brand's identity and its worth. So these inputs need to be taken very seriously if the brand wants to survive the test of time. The brand needs to build its external identity, giving a hard look at various facets – including the way boutique managers are handling customers, post-sale customer service as well a brand campaign, or the selection of brand ambassadors.

It is the marriage of the external and internal identities that make a luxury brand stand the test of time.

Chapter 19

The Luxe Legacy

The key to creating luxe is 'aspiration'. Brand custodians have one, all-focussed task at hand – to create aspiration. The craving of a consumer to be associated with a brand is the key to his wallet or her purse. And 'brand legacy' is a fail-safe mechanism for creating desire and dazzle.

Legacy typically means 'inheritance', something passed on from one generation to next. There is a sense of exclusivity to the whole notion of legacy. This exclusivity and a desire to belong to a certain legacy give the opportunity to a brand to create an 'aspirational quotient'.

Imagine yourself using a luggage brand that was once exclusively used by the Maharajas. Or imagine wearing a watch brand that was worn by legendary leaders such as JFK. You feel that a part of you is connected to that legacy that has a high 'aspirational quotient'. It is almost as if the earlier generation of royalty or legends have passed on to your generation, to you. Such is the high of exclusivity, in turn, establishing an instant connect of the brand with the consumer.

Talking of royalties, let me elaborate with an example of the palaces. Let's take the case of the beautiful and exquisite Lake Palace, which is now with Taj Lake Palace Udaipur. With its guest list including Queen Elizabeth, former first lady Jacqueline Kennedy, Shah of Iran, Lord Kurzon and Vivian Leigh, it is no wonder that they charge 20,000 USD per night on average. Or take the example of the Raj Palace of Jaipur, which charges a tariff as high as 50,000 USD. Royal Suite of Raj Palace is the second-most expensive suite in the world. Now these are real palaces, which companies have converted into hotels.

The service in these 'palace hotels' is aligned to the service that Maharajas used to receive. Once you spend time in these palaces and drink from a gold glass, or eat from a gold plate, or admire the real gold used in decorating a wall, the entire ambiance is created, may be overdone, in such a way to dazzle you and make you feel 'privileged' in the company of royalty. Soon you realize that you are really living a life of a Maharaja, and it does not require any bloodline anymore. It is like an inheritance, a legacy. These hotels thrive on the aspirational quotient and thus essentially on legacy of the 'Brand Royalty'.

Now, will a seasoned hotel brand like Taj be able to charge the same premium by 'creating a palace'? The answer is no. The reason being a lack of history. The fact that these 'palaces' have a history and thus a legacy, already nudges the consumers to loosen their purse strings. What adds to the premium is the way royalty is showcased with the opulence so as to recreate the times of the Maharajas.

Watch brands like IWC also boast of Presidents wearing their watch and thus of legacy. However, Rolex takes the cake here. The former being more exclusive and Rolex being more inclusive, the appeal of legacy of Rolex reaches far and wide. And so, it can easily accommodate a Roger Federer in the "Live for Greatness" campaign along with JFK and Martin Luther King Jr.

Thus, a brand custodian needs to evaluate the brand and understand how a legacy needs to be marketed well so that it does not end up alienating people. So if a group of potential buyers are not encouraged to be a part of the legacy of JFK, they might fall for Federer.

Let your quest for luxe legacy continue.

Chapter 20

Philosophy behind Branding Desire

When you hear the name of a particular luxury brand, what is the first thought? The answer is, it depends. The images that are already conjured by the custodians, who brand desire as well as your personal experiences with the brand, are responsible for bringing up these first thoughts. So in one part, it is the real experience, and on the other, the imaginative faculty that the brand is able to successfully arouse. In this mix of fact and fiction, what really transpires is very personal. If your experience is good or if it had left a sour taste will finally determine the outcome. On the surface, every luxury brand aims to give a sense of exclusivity and class. It is a tool to make you feel special. And the premium charged is just a means to an end.

So what exactly is the philosophy behind branding desire? Essentially it means the promise that a brand makes to its customers. Let me explore some facets of brand philosophy:

Brand existence: The first critical piece behind brand philosophy is the prime reason behind its existence, the raison d'être. Why do we need that brand in an already cluttered brand-verse? The brand needs to find the reason of its existence and establish it in the eyes of the customers.

Brand positioning: After establishing its reason for existence, and once the brand itself is convinced on its existence, it is time to find a niche and establish itself in the eyes of its customers. So now, from the brand's eyes to the customer's eyes, the brand is finally able to establish its niche.

Brand story: The third component of the philosophy is the brand story. This is the time when the custodians have their creative juices flowing. This is the best way to establish the brand philosophy to the customers. For example, if the brand philosophy is to live the core values, then the story has to be built around how the brand actually is walking the talk and not just doing lip service. The brand campaigns, which are used to tell this story, have to be clear in their narrative as to how a brand is living up to its philosophy.

Brand communication: Taking the story across various media helps communicate the brand story to the target audience. A brand needs to identify the right format and the right media for communicating its story to establish its philosophy. For example, if a luxury brand wants to reach out to a young audience, then the preferred format will be videos as opposed to a print ad, which is more suited for a more mature clientele. Similarly, the media chosen for a young audience will be social media versus a magazine for more mature clients. These choices are the reasons why communication is impactful or it fails to resonate with the audience.

Brand touch points: No matter how successfully a brand is able to communicate its philosophy, sloppy handling of a client can make or break its reputation. Be it an inappropriate gesture at a boutique by a rookie or by an over-smart manager, or even a rude customer care executive over a phone call, it will do more harm than a brand custodian can ever imagine. It is the 'fact' that I was talking about, that with the sprinkled 'fiction', will

conjure up the real philosophy in the minds of
the customers.

'Lost are we, and are only so far punished,
That without hope we live on in desire.'

The Death Mask of
King Tut-Ankh-Amun

Tailpiece

Sustainable luxury is the new mantra

My message is that we'll be watching you. This is all wrong. I shouldn't be up here. I should be back in school on the other side of the ocean. Yet, you all come to us young people for hope. How dare you?

– Greta Thunberg

This is the message of the future generation. And the answer lies in sustainability, in caring for them. Like Greta, millennials too take a lead towards this change. The millennial millionaires are more conscious of the environmental and social impact of their purchase decisions and are more likely to buy from a brand that resonates with their own personal values. Therefore, brands which want to retain their status in the luxury market need to evolve to keep up with this growing trend towards ethical and sustainable luxury.

According to a Nielsen survey, 73% of millennials respondents were willing to spend more on a product if it comes from a sustainable or socially conscious brand. Furthermore, 81% of millennials expect the brands that they buy to be transparent in their marketing and actively talk about their sustainability impact. Nielsen dubbed 2018 as the Year of the Influential Sustainability Consumer – nearly half of the consumers say they would change their habits to reduce their impact on the environment.

Luxury is all about time. The time spent in handcrafting, tweaking with precision in transforming a product from ordinary to exquisite. It is now time to take the narrative further and bring in sustainability in this business of luxury. A new breed of innovative thinkers see sustainability as a driver of, rather than a brake on, innovation.

Designers at LVMH Moët Hennessy are heavily investing in new materials to replace plastic and improve leather tanning. This move towards sustainability cuts costs and boosts profits whilst benefiting the planet.

The Kering group, for example, which owns Gucci, Stella McCartney, and Saint Laurent, among other high-end labels, is increasing the share of its raw materials that are renewable to improve its sustainability.

Chanel banned use of exotic leather as a step towards ethical sourcing and invested in developing biodegradable plastic. Chanel decided to share its sustainability story with everyone.

Branding sustainable luxury

Once we have an idea of the new marriage between sustainability and luxury, let us now understand how a luxury brand needs to market itself to reach out to the target audience as an icon of social responsibility.

Just a word of caution to the luxury brands – if some brands try to join this bandwagon of sustainability to catch the young consumers and build their brand without genuinely implementing sustainability and environmentally-friendly models into their practice from the ground up, it will be detrimental for their reputation.

So the effort needs to be genuine and not superficial. Therefore, the communication and branding has to be subtle and not over the top. The millennial millionaires are smart enough to know whether a brand is 'using' sustainability to bait them and deep inside are not socially responsible. 'How dare you?' They will shout like Greta.

If luxury brands want to win over the affluent millennials, they have to be socially responsible and create a positive environmental impact.

One good example of branding is by Rolex. The Rolex Award for Enterprise, the company gives a large cash prize to entrepreneurs between the ages of 18 and 30 years for projects that are bringing about a positive environmental or cultural change. This approach towards sustainable luxury and socially conscious innovation is an innovative branding tool.

Brands can also actively campaign for bringing about a change. These campaigns, with the right intent, are great opportunities to create the right association of a luxury brand with sustainability.

Even small steps such as doing away with plastic bags and replacing them with

environment-friendly cloth or paper or jute bags
are also lauded by consumers.

Communication and branding is a subtle art
when it comes to showcasing such sensitive
matters which impact our future generations.
Therefore, any luxury brand, that wants to
survive the test of time, needs to subtly bring in
sustainability in its narrative.

Let your quest for luxe never end!

Praise for The Z of Marketing

Totally unconventional, Kingsley challenges all the myths creating fear in the heart of modern day marketers. The perfect practical approach for the developing world.
Lawal Babatope Alex,
Serial Entrepreneur

Incisive, practical and dynamic, The Z of Marketing will inspire you, elevate you and teach you. Everyone who desires to move their business to another level should read this book.
Sunny Agboju
CEO, Prot Consulting Ltd

"The Z of Marketing" is a practical "how to" list of key principles applied by the author that will work for any SME that faithfully implements and practices thereby changing the narrative of the failure of most SME's in these climes. I look forward to many organizations transiting from SME's to World class multinationals as a result of this book.
Demola Onanuga
ED/CEO, Basscomm Group

If you are looking for proven marketing tips, "The Z of Marketing" is a must.
JuwonLawal
MD/CEO, ABD Fuels Ltd

1

The Z of MARKETING
How I Get Rapid Sales & How You Too Can

KINGSLEY AIGBONA
Creator of "The WOW-Factor Staff"

Go beyond theory. Learn down to earth easy-to-understand
practical principles on getting and keeping clients/customers

---